# THE LAST DAYS OF KRISHNA AND THE SONS OF PANDU

# THE LAST DAYS OF KRISHNA AND THE SONS OF PANDU:

FROM THE

CONCLUDING SECTION OF THE MAHABHARAT

TRANSLATOR

NEKKEIB KHAN, DAVID PRICE

GYAN

*Published by*

Gyan Publishing House
5, Ansari Road
Daryaganj, New Delhi-110002
Phone: 011-47034999, 9811692060
E-mail: books@gyanbooks.com

*Distribution Network*
gyanbooks.com
India, USA, Canada, UK, Australia



ISBN: 978-93-6920-684-1 (PB)

First Published, 1835

2nd Impression 2025

*Printed at:* Gyan Press, Delhi.



**THE LAST DAYS OF KRISHNA AND THE SONS OF PANDU**
Translator: NEKKEIB KHAN, DAVID PRICE

# THE LAST DAYS OF KRISHNA AND THE SONS OF PANDU,

FROM THE

## CONCLUDING SECTION OF THE MAHABHARAT.

---

TRANSLATED FROM THE PERSIAN VERSION,

MADE BY

NEKKEIB KHAN,

IN THE TIME OF THE EMPEROR AKBAR,

BY

MAJOR DAVID PRICE,

OF THE BOMBAY ARMY;

*Member of the Royal Asiatic Society; of the Oriental Translation Committee; and of the Royal Society of Literature.*

THE

# LAST DAYS OF KRISHNA

AND

# THE SONS OF PANDU

FROM

## THE CONCLUDING SECTIONS OF THE MAHABHARAT.*

---

The authors to whom we are indebted for our information on the subject of this eventful story, continue their relation in the following terms:—After his stupendous victory over Jerjudehn† and the sons of Kourû,‡ Rajah Judishter,§ and his four brothers, continued to exercise the sovereign power without competition, for a period of six and thirty years. At the expiration of that period, several omens of an inauspicious character began, however, to make their appearance. Furious and adverse winds arose, driving before them even stones and rocks; animals, whose appearance on the right hand betokened good fortune, exhibited themselves on the sinister quarter, and such as ought to have appeared to the left, passed upon the right: the waters ascended contrary

* مهابهارت † جرجودهن ‡ کوروان § راجه جدشتر

to their course; the sky rained fire, and ashes, and half-burnt cinders; at other times, in a perfect calm, and when it could not have been occasioned by the march of armies, or other multitudinous bodies, clouds of dust arose in such masses as to obscure the light of the sun: it afforded neither light nor radiance; and around that luminary, also, might be observed what had the appearance of a stupendous dome,* or arch, and on every side of it a circle of dark stars, or shots, in the very middle of the day; these were followed, at intervals, by other portents which fill the hearts of men with sorrow and alarm.

The sons of Pandû,† and the whole of the people subject to their authority, thrown into consternation by the appearance of these prodigies, became assured that they must prognosticate some fearful calamities; and it was at such a crisis, (while the illustrious members of the family were one day seated in the midst of their nobles) that a person arrived from Duarka,‡ with intelligence that the Jadous,§ the kindred of Krishna,‖ so called, had been drawn into civil conflict, and had all perished by the sword. The Rajah, and his people, were overwhelmed with affliction by the intelligence; and the following day, having called together the great men of the country, the Rajah proceeded to state to them the

* كنبذ † پاندوان ‡ دواركا

§ جادوان perhaps Magi. ‖ كرشن

accounts which had reached him, testifying equal grief and apprehension, lest some fearful calamity might have happened to their adored Krishna. Several of these grandees expressed an opinion that such information was not to be relied upon, considering it very improbable that any events of such a nature should have occurred when Krishna was present. They therefore intreated him to calm his apprehensions until the truth should be ascertained. To put the matter out of doubt, Rajah Judishter accordingly signified a desire that some person might be dispatched to Duarka, in order to obtain positive information as to the state of affairs with Krishna, his brother Balbehdder,* and the rest of the family.

Here Rajah Jemenjah† demanded of Bishempayina,‡ what it was that could have occasioned this unnatural and sanguinary conflict among the Jadous, notwithstanding the presence of such a leader as Kessou.§ When six and thirty years had expired of the reign of Judishter, and the sons of Pandû, replied the sage, in consequence of the malediction of certain Brahmins,

* بلبهدر

† راجہ جمنجے N.B. This personage appears to have been the third or fourth in descent from Krishna, and the narrative is carried on in a dialogue between him and his instructor, who was a disciple of Beyaussa, the author of the Mahabharat.

‡ بشمپاین

§ کیسو one of Krishna's thousand names.

those fatal hostilities arose among the Jadous, which terminated in the destruction of the whole race: and being further requested to explain by whom it was that the malediction was uttered, which could have produced such a calamitous result, Bishempayina proceeded to relate as follows:—Biswamitra,* Derbaussa,† and Nareda,‡ all of them Rehkkisers,§ or ascetics of the highest class, so much so, that from head to foot they were one body of devotion and abstinence, happened on a time to be sitting together in meditation on the perfections of the Supreme Being. It also happened that Sârum‖ the son of Basdeu,¶ and Samenba,** or Samenpet, the son of Krishna, accompanied by a crowd of boys of the Jadou nation, in pursuit of amusement, came to the spot where the three ascetics had secluded themselves. As soon as the young people saw who they were, they put the son of Krishna into the disguise of a young woman, and leading him so disguised into the presence of the three Brahmins, they stated that this person was the wife of one of the Jadou tribe, and that being pregnant, they were desirous of learning from them, what from their exalted character they could doubtless be able to decide, the nature of the issue to which she was destined to give birth.

" We are not ignorant," said the Rehkkisers, " whom

* بسوامتر † درباسا ‡ نارد § رکهیسران

‖ سارن ¶ باسدیو ** سامنب

it is that you have attempted to impose upon us as a female; we know it to be the son of Krishna: that to which he shall give birth will be a wedge of iron, destined to be an instrument of destruction to the whole race of Jadou. Now we repeat, that since, instead of a virtuous life, you have preferred a course of evil; since, on scoffing at and turning into ridicule such harmless and defenceless objects as we are, you have given abundant proof of the pride and arrogance with which you are animated, it behoves you to remember, this same wedge, or piece of iron, as surely as we have foretold it, will be instrumental to your destruction, and that of the whole of your race, Krishna and Balbehdder alone excepted. Neither will they be permitted long to survive; for soon after the catastrophe, Balbehdder will be called upon to quit this mortal form, and pass into the ocean; and Krishna himself shall leave the world."

Having thus said, the three Rehkkisers arose together, and throwing the deer-skins on which they had been seated across their shoulders, withdrew from Duarka, making the best of their way towards Hastnapour,* to the province of Rajah Judishter, where in due time they arrived in safety. The youths of Duarka, on the other hand, grieved beyond measure at what they had

* هستناپور on the Ganges, the ancient capital of the sons of Bharat.

heard from the three Brahmins, and deeply regretting what they had done, returned to their homes in the city. The circumstance in a short time became known among the inhabitants, and occasioned some alarming apprehensions. Krishna was also apprized of the portentous prediction, and his observation was, that whatever was the will of God would surely come to pass. He said no more, and betook himself to his home.

The very next day, or very shortly afterwards, a piece of iron, of the precise description foretold by the Brahmins, was discharged from the bowels of Sampa or Samba, that very thing which was to consummate the doom of the race of Jadou. In shape, it was similar to the club made use of, and wielded round the head, by Athletæ,* and others whose profession it is to exhibit feats of strength.

The appearance of this prodigy was early reported to Oukra Sing,† who directed his smiths to take the ominous substance in hand, and by filing reduce it to nothing. They accordingly set to work, and scattering the filings among the sands on the sea shore, continued to make use of these files, until the substance became something less than the palm of a man's hand; but when they found that all their endeavours to reduce it

* كشتي كير

† اوكرسين the reigning sovereign of Duarka.

to a smaller size were unavailing, they cast the remaining part into the sea. The filings which they had thrown among the sands produced a sea weed,* or something of that kind growing along the sea shore.

This done, it was proclaimed throughout the city, that Rajah Oukra Sing, and Krishna, and Balbehdder, had joined to prohibit the use of inebriating liquors, under the penalty of death; it being, at the same time, announced that any person detected in transgressing this ordinance of the reigning powers would be impaled alive, together with all his family. Hence, as might have been expected, the people very generally abstained from drinking, their terror of detection being so great, that they durst not even pronounce the very name of the proscribed beverage.

Not long afterwards, there was seen a fearful apparition, in the form of a human being, whose complexion was a mixture of black and yellow, his head bald, and all his limbs distorted, supposed to be the angel of death,† prowling about Duarká, and presenting himself at the doors of the inhabitants, to their infinite dismay and terror. Nevertheless, when assailed by their arrows, the apparition vanished in a manner that none could ever tell what it was, or whither it went.

Tremendous hurricanes then arose, tearing up whole forests by the root, and carrying away both man and beast. The dwellings of the inhabitants became infested

* پُوج　　† موت

with rats to such a degree, that thousands of thousands filled every house; in short, nothing could be laid aside for keeping that they did not either carry off or destroy. The market places were completely over-run by these pestilent animals, which eat off even the hair and beards of the men, while asleep. The nightingale and the Sharek* were both scared by the noise of the rats, and the hootings of the owl, and continued their wailings both night and day. The owls flocked to the houses also in immense numbers, filling the air from night to morning with their doleful cries from the terraces.

The time was also remarkable for monstrous births in a variety of shapes: kine brought forth asses; swine brought forth colts; dogs produced cats and weazels, rats or mice. Vice and profligacy in every shape, and to an alarming degree, pervaded the whole race of Jadou. The poor man and the devotee were equally exposed to every species of abuse. Neither learning, nor the instructors of youth, were any longer the object of respect. Men were over-ruled by women; fire gave no light, and flame burnt black and blue. The sun at rising and setting was surrounded by thousands of thousands of headless human forms,† which, sword and spear in hand, appeared engaged in mortal conflict, the whole

* شارک a sort of nightingale. I have thought it to have been the miner, a well known talking bird in India.

† تول or راسو

people contemplating the fearful spectacle with astonishment and consternation.

The skins employed to repose upon by Joguies and other devotees, they found, if quitted even for the shortest interval, changed into maggots, or other vermin. The moon was eclipsed* on its twelfth day, and the sun on the twenty-seventh day of the moon. Observing this latter phenomenon, Krishna remarked, that these untimely eclipses of the sun and moon had occurred before during the war of the Mahabarat, and this was the second instance, in a period of six and thirty years which had since elapsed. At that time, he said, a curse had been imprecated upon him by Kandahâry,† for the part he had taken in the death of Jurjudehn and the sons of Kourû. Prodigies such as these, he added, occurred at the crisis of the destruction of that race, and their present occurrence probably foreboded some similar catastrophe.

On a subsequent night a proclamation was issued by Krishna, that the whole of the people should repair on the following morning to the sea-shore, there to perform a service of devotion to the deity‡ they worshipped. That same night there appeared at Duarka a black woman, clothed also in black, with yellow teeth. This apparition went from house to house grinning at the inhabitants to their infinite dismay, and when they

* Qr. كرفت‌شد † كاندهاري ‡ تيرت يعني معبد

attempted to seize it vanishing from one place to shew itself at another, until it had made a circuit of the whole city. The jewels of the women and the arms of the men were at the same time carried off by evil spirits, without the possibility of recovery. The Chakra* or discus of Krishna, was taken up to heaven in sight of the people, who gave way to the loudest expression of grief on the occasion. Dâreka,† the elephant driver‡ of Krishna, having harnessed the horses to the car of his master, the animals made a sudden spring, and bearing the car into the air, crossed the sea, and disappeared for ever.

The device on the standard of Balbehdder, the brother of Krishna, was a taur,§ or toddy palm, and that on the standard of Krishna was a symourg, or phœnix; both these figures were suddenly seen to separate from the standards on which they were delineated, and rising into the air, vanished from the sight for ever. Voices were also heard in the air, calling upon the people to be "up and away." Similar voices were heard also in the dwellings of the inhabitants.

In obedience to this proclamation of Krishna, the inhabitants of Duarka proceeded on the day proposed to the sea shore, by every species of conveyance, and provided in splendid abundance with every requisite to testify their devotion to the god of their adoration. On

* چکر † دارک ‡ Qr. بهلبان § تار

that very day a personage of the highest distinction among the race of Jadou, who bore the name of Oudhou,* and who was without a rival in prudence, piety, and every virtue that could adorn the mind, unexpectedly besought and obtained the permission of Krishna, to withdraw into the northern regions. This person is said, through the intensity of his devotion, to have become so enrobed in light, that the spot where he stood appeared illuminated as if it were the effect of fire.

When, on this occasion, the people had taken their places in the order arranged for them, they were directed by Krishna, as an indispensable preliminary, to make a distribution to the Brahmins of every kind of refreshment, meat, and drink, and confectionary. When these refreshments had been properly arranged, a certain individual of the Jadou tribe, carrying in his hand a jar of liquor, had indulged to such excess, that he became brutally intoxicated; and in this state, pouring a small quantity of the liquor into the palm of his hand, he dared to sprinkle it over the food intended for the Brahmins: the latter, of course, abstained with abhorrence from tasting any part of it; and Krishna, in consequence, directed that the whole should be thrown to the monkeys.

The jugglers and singers, the music both vocal and instrumental, now struck up on every side, and the whole

* اودهو

of the people, who in consequence of the prohibition had abstained for some time from the use of liquor, now that they had received permission, proceeded to indulge themselves without restraint. The divine Krishna, on his part, presided over a splendid circle, composed of whatever was noble and illustrious among the race of Jadou. Such were Oukra Sing, the reigning chief, and Balbehdder the elder brother of Krishna and Beyrû,* and Sautek, and Kerretburma,† and Purdeman,‡ and Nesset,§ the sons of Krishna, and numerous others who graced this magnificent assembly with their presence; and but few of any name among the tribe were absent on this occasion. When the assemblage seemed complete, and the different chiefs had taken their places, Balbehdder, who as already noticed, was the elder brother of Krishna, and who is described as the grand promoter of drinking, now gave orders that jars of wine or other liquors should be brought in, and arranged before the several guests, who immediately formed into small separate parties, for the better convenience of social conversation. Thus Balbehdder and Kerretburmâ sat together; Purdeman with Sautek and Serna,‖ the younger brother of Krishna.

Of these, Sautek becoming early intoxicated, and directing his eye towards Kerretburma, called to his friends to observe the insolence of that boastful and arrogant

* بیرو † کرت‌برما ‡ پردمن § نست ‖ سرنا

Tchetry,* dilating on the exploits performed by himself and Ashoutehâma,† against a band of beardless boys, and the glory of having butchered so many undefending mendicants. Purdeman loudly applauded the remark of his brother; and Kerretburma, by this time also considerably heated with what he had been drinking, addressed himself to Sautek, and demanded if it became him to be sarcastic, or to indulge in such remarks, who had stolen the light of Serwaudet.‡ Here Krishna beckoning to Sautek, hinted to him to relate the fact of Kerretburma having murdered Setrâjut,§ and robbed of the mysterious jewels, of which he was the possessor. The circumstance of this transaction are then described in the following terms.

Setrâjut was a person of the Jadou tribe, who had a younger brother of the name of Bebber Sing.‖ The former had distinguished himself in an eminent degree by his zeal in the adoration of the sun, and that luminary was so attracted by the fervour of his devotion, that it bestowed upon him a gem of such transcendant lustre as to rival its own radiance.

* جهتري † اشوتهامار ‡ سروادت

§ ستراجت N.B. It is remarkable that the exterminating war of the Mahabharat, and the slaughter at Duarka, should have originated, the former in a gambling transaction, and the latter in a drunken debauch.

‖ ببرسين

Setrâjut suspended this unrivalled jewel to his neck, and as he was on some occasion proceeding on a visit to Krishna, and such a splendor was diffused around him, that the attendants concurred it could be no other than the sun himself coming to see their master, and so announced him. Krishna told them with a smile, that it was not indeed the sun, but Setrâjut, and that the surprising radiance which they had observed, was produced by a jewel which he wore on his neck, and which had been presented to him by the sun. When accordingly Setrâjut had entered, and seated himself among them, they began to interrogate him them on the subject of his extraordinary gem, and he told them without hesitation that it was a present from the luminary which he adored; neither did he conceal from them some miraculous properties which belonged to it: such as that it gave to the ground on which it beamed the value of twenty ass loads of gold; that it protected the person who bore it from pain and affliction, and from the bite or sting of snake and scorpion, and every other noxious reptile whatever. It possessed many other virtues, which he did not, he said, think it necessary to enumerate; but he had already said enough to awaken the wonder and admiration of his hearers.

Having left the presence of Krishna, Setrâjut returned home; and shortly afterwards he received a message from Krishna, importing that Oukra Sing, their common chief, had signified his desire to be possessed of the jewel, and advising him, as it was an article of such extraordinary rarity that crowned heads were alone worthy of its possession, to send it to the presence without delay. The answer of Setrâjut was conceived in the following terms:

"You have every thing at command; but as for me, after years of devotion to the sun, this jewel has been bestowed upon me, as a proof of the approbation of the deity whom I adore, and while I have life I will never resign it to any one."

This reply was conveyed to Krishna, and he said no more on the subject.

One day, however, the brother of Setrâjut, the Bebber Sing above noticed, took it into his head to place this jewel on his neck, and having mounted his horse, and paraded some time before the entrance of Krishna's dwelling, rode out to hunt on the neighbouring plains; but here a lion crossed his path, and although he drew his sword to defend himself, with a stroke of his paw killed him on the spot. Seeing the jewel at his neck, the lordly animal seized it with its mouth, and went its way. It had not, however, proceeded far, when it met with a bear, and in the conflict which ensued the lion was killed. The jewel thus came into possession of the bear, by which it was conveyed to its den. As many days now passed without any intelligence of Bebber Sing, people did not scruple to assert that Krishna had murdered him, and stolen the jewel.

The foul slander which was in circulation against him, was communicated to Krishna, and excited the deepest indignation in his bosom. Forthwith taking with him some of the most expert tracers of game, he followed the footmarks left by Bebber Sing's horse, until he came to the spot where lay the rider's lifeless body, with every indication that he had been slain by a wild beast. The track of the lion was sufficiently distinct, and they followed it carefully to the spot where they found the carcase. They lastly traced the footmarks of the bear until they came to the mouth of a large cavern on the side of a mountain. Here Krishna told his attendants that he should enter the cavern alone, where probably he should find the jewel of which they were in search.

From this they in vain endeavoured to dissuade him, as he persisted in his determination, directing them to remain at the entrance of the cavern for twelve days, and if at the termination of that period they saw nothing of him, they might return to Duarka.

Krishna entered the cavern accordingly, and having proceeded some distance within, the first object he beheld was a female of exquisite beauty, seated by a cradle containing an infant child, and above the cradle was suspended the jewel of which he was in search. As soon as she saw the intruder, the female uttered a loud cry, which reaching the ears of the bear Jamounet, or Jamounta,* who was the father of the damsel, the latter

* جامونت

rushed to the spot and commenced a furious combat with Krishna, which was continued, with little intermission, for a period of eight and twenty days. On the eight and twentieth day, however, victory declared for Krishna; his antagonist, in acknowledging his defeat, assuring him that, with the exception of Rama, he had never before met with a conqueror. Now, therefore, that he had experienced the matchless power of his arm, he had no difficulty in giving him the glory, he besought him to pursue his vengeance no further, for that he submitted to become his vassal. Krishna forebore accordingly from further molestation, and Jamounta, together with his beautiful daughter whom he presented to him for his wife, delivered to him the mysterious gem, the object of such avidity, with a variety of other precious rarities, of which he thus made an offering to his conqueror.

Krishna, with his new bride, the jewel, and other rarities, now quitted the cavern of Jamounta; his attendants having departed, when, at the expiration of twelve days, they found that he did not return according to promise. On reaching Duarka, they communicated all that they knew of the fate of Krishna, to his father Basdeu, to his brother Balbehdder, and to his wives and children, and other relatives; and his disappearance produced in the whole of Duarka the deepest sorrow and affliction. Setrâjut and his brothers were exposed to the most bitter reproaches, as having by these slanderous reports occasioned the distress; and they were preparing to mourn for his loss, when to their universal delight their favourite Krishna appeared once more among them.

The people of Duarka being now called together by Krishna, he delivered to Setrâjut, in the presence of the whole assembly, the jewel which had occasioned such unjust suspicions; the men who had attended him in his search, bearing testimony to all the circumstances which had been discovered of the fate of Bebber Sing; his death by the lion, and the death of the lion by the bear. Setrâjut expressed the deepest regret for the suspicions which he had so unjustly entertained of the conduct of Krishna, at whose feet he now fell imploring forgiveness: and as some atonement for what had happened, together with the mysterious jewel, offered him the hand of his daughter Setbahamah.* Krishna accepted of the damsel, but declined the jewel altogether.

At a subsequent period, while Krishna was absent on a visit to the sons of Pandû, at Hastnapour, Kerretburma, availing himself of the opportunity, employed his brother Setdeu,† one night to murder Setrâjut, and bring away the solar gem. Setbahâmah, the daughter of Setrâjut and wife of Krishna, having caused the body of her father to be preserved in a vessel of oil, made the best of her way to Hastnapour, where with bitter lamentation she announced to her husband the murder of her father. Immediately calling for his charger,‡ and

* ستبهامه

† ستديو

‡ كرت

mounting, with Setbahamah behind him, he proceeded on his return to Duarka.

The brother of Kerretburma, apprized of the approach of Krishna, and aware that the murder of Setrâjut would be fearfully avenged upon him, consigned the jewel to another brother of the name of Egrour,* or perhaps Egrider, and mounting a mare of matchless speed, betook himself to flight. Krishna, on his part, hearing of the flight of Setdeu, again mounted the same charger, and taking his brother Balbehdder along with him, set off in pursuit of the fugitive. Having rode four hundred kôsse on the same day, and his mare being disabled from going any longer, Setdeu was compelled to dismount, and continue his flight on foot. Soon afterwards Krishna came up, and finding that the fugitive had quitted his mare, also dismounted, and continued the pursuit on foot. As he ran eagerly along, he soon overtook the murderer, and with a single stroke of his chakra severed his head from the body: but although every part of his vesture was carefully examined, not a vestige of the jewel could be discovered.

Shortly afterwards, Balbehdder also came up, and abruptly demanded of his brother what he had done with the jewel: Krishna truly replied, that after the minutest search he had not been able to find any thing of it. Hence, conceiving a suspicion that his brother had in-

* اکرور

tentionally secreted the jewel, Balbehdder became displeased; and immediately separating from Krishna, withdrew towards Terhut,* at this period under the dominion of a certain Rajah Chung.† The latter conducted him to his palace with every demonstration of respect, and there he continued to be hospitably entertained for a considerable time. At this crisis, Rajah Jerjudehn was residing at Hastnapour, and hearing that Balbehdder had taken up his abode at Terhut, also repaired to that place; where he long remained under the tuition of Balbehdder, by whom he was instructed in the use of the mace, war club, or battle axe.

On his separation from Balbehdder, Krishna returned to Duarka; from whence, when he heard of his approach, after having slain his brother, Ekrour now fled with precipitation, taking away with him the innocent cause of these jealousies, the precious solar gem. The flight of this personage was succeeded by a long and distressing drought at Duarka, in consequence of a malediction which, on her grief at his absence, his mother had prevailed upon a certain devotee to invoke upon the land. When the rains had been thus for a long time alarmingly withheld from the country, the people presented themselves before Krishna, and implored relief. Krishna, impelled by the extremity, sent messengers to recal the fugitive, and such was the language

* ترهت † جنگ

of conciliation employed, that he was finally prevailed upon to return to Duarka; and then, on being conducted to the presence of Krishna, after many apologies, he offered to place in his hands the much contested jewel. Krishna, however, again declined acceptance, and returned it to Ekrour.

Basdeu, the father of Krishna, when it was ascertained that the jewel was still in the possession of Ekrour, dispatched without delay a request to Balbehdder, that he would return to Duarka; and the messengers being at the same time charged with explanations from Krishna on the subject of the jewel, Balbehdder became ashamed of his unjust suspicions, and returned accordingly to Duarka, where, through the intervention of their common father Basdeu, he became cordially reconciled to his brother, with whom he continued to a distant period to live on terms of the greatest amity, and in every species of enjoyment.

Resuming the subject, from which the above is so large a digression, the historian proceeds to relate, that when, during the angry discussion between Sautek and Kerretburma, Krishna demanded, with some asperity, of the former why he hesitated to repeat the story of Setrâjut, Setbahâmah, the daughter of that personage and wife of Krishna, bursting into tears at the name of her father, placed herself before Krishna, and indignantly demanded, if then it was with his permission that these men had murdered her father? Krishna spoke not a word;

but Sautek arose, and addressing Setbahâmah, desired her to suspend her grief, for that he would amply avenge upon these miscreants the blood of her father. "This Kerretburma," continued he, "is the man that, in conjunction with Ashutâhama, unjustly slew the son of Droopede and Sekahnde,* with Dereshtedeman,† and so many thousand more blameless and innocent individuals. Their years are numbered; and for the blood thus cruelly shed, will I exact the most awful account." Having thus said, he drew his sword, and advanced towards Kerretburma; the latter also placed his hand upon his sword, and was in the act of rising from his seat, when with one unerring sweep of the sword of Sautek his head fell to the ground.

Several of the kindred of Kerretburma now rushed upon Sautek, and many of them fell by his hand. Those who sought to avenge the death of that chief were, however, formidable in numbers; and as their attack was exclusively directed towards his destroyer, the friends of Sautek were not less eager to hasten to his support. At such a crisis, observing that the uproar was assuming a very alarming appearance, Krishna arose and endeavoured to pacify or allay the fury of the combatants; but neither command nor remonstrance was availing. The relations of Kerretburma continued to press upon Sautek; and although his brother Purdaman

* سهکندي

† درشتدمن

rushed courageously to his assistance, and put to death many of his assailants, the two gallant brothers were finally overpowered, and slain in the very presence of Krishna. The rage of the latter was now fully excited, and he arose to avenge the death of his sons.

It appears that on this occasion Krishna was entirely unarmed, and the only substitute that offered was the sea-weed already noticed, which grew among the sands. Some of this he now tore up, and with it smote the destroyers of his children, all whom he could reach dying on the spot. Others now flew to assail the life of Krishna, but all who approached within the sweep of his branch of sea-weed, fell to rise no more. The people in general now ran to furnish themselves with this singular material for slaughter, and armed with this alone rushed to mutual destruction, inevitable death awaiting all that came within its reach; father against son, and son against father, and brother against brother, and kindred of every degree against kindred, combated with the same material, until all perished to the last man. Such in short was the fatal result of the malediction of the three Rehkkisers.

In this tumultuous conflict fell, among thousands of others, the sons and grandsons of Krishna; whose affliction it would be difficult to describe, when he beheld among the slain the mangled bodies of his sons Purdaman, and Samba, and Chardepas,* and the son of

* چاردپس

Purdaman, Anerdeha,* and Gada,† another of the brothers of Krishna, including the greater part of his illustrious kindred. While thus absorbed in sorrowful contemplation of the spectacle before him, Dârek, the charioteer of Krishna, intimated to his lord, that just as the tumult was commencing, he observed his brother Balbehdder quit the assembly and disappear. Peradventure, he said, the calamity which proved fatal to so many others might have extended also to him. Aroused by the hint, Krishna directed that his car might be brought, and mounting forthwith, accompanied by Beir,‡ another of the chiefs of the Jadou tribe, and his charioteer seated in front, proceeded in quest of Balbehdder. They had not proceeded far when they discovered him of whom they were in search, seated under the shade of a Bur, or Banyan tree, with his eyes closed, and totally absorbed in meditation.

Krishna and his companion approached in silence, and quietly seated themselves beside him, his thoughts being so entirely engrossed on other objects, that he seemed unconscious that any one was by. Here Krishna addressing himself to the charioteer, said, " Thou hast witnessed all that has befallen this people; begone, therefore, and make the best of thy way to Hastnapour, to the presence of Rajah Judishter, acquaint him with all that thou hath seen, and intreat that Arjun may as

* انردها † كد

‡ بیرجادوان The Pair or patron saint of the sons of Jadou. Qu.

soon as possible be sent to Duarka." Dârek, accordingly, mounting the car of his master, proceeded with all speed in his power to Hastnapour.

On the departure of Dârek, Krishna turning to the Jadou chief, by whom he was accompanied, said that he also had been a sorrowful witness of the recent disastrous scenes. It was his request now, that he would immediately return to the city to provide for the protection of their dwellings, lest a lawless banditti, taking advantage of the absence of its defenders, might pillage the place and abuse the women. He added, that his father Basdeu, who had not quitted Duarka on the day of the disaster, would also require his attention. As he was hastening towards Duarka, however, this Beir, or whatever else was his name, was encountered by a drunken fisherman, who beat him to death with a bunch of the fatal sea weed. The circumstance having, by some means or other, been made known to Krishna, he then said to Balbehdder, that as he was apprehensive that the city might be exposed to injury from lawless depredations, it was indispensably necessary that he should repair to Duarka. He requested, however, that Balbehdder would remain where he was, without stirring from the spot, until his return, which he assured him would not be delayed a moment longer than was necessary.

Returning to Duarka accordingly, Krishna hastened to the presence of his father, who was now, for the first time, made acquainted with the awful story of that sanguinary and unnatural conflict which had involved the race of Jadou in total destruction. The venerable *Basdeu,* on information of the disaster which had thus bereaved him of so many cherished relatives and friends, became overwhelmed with sorrow, to which he gave expression in the bitterest lamentation. "Alas, my father," interrupted Krishna, "the calamity which we deplore may indeed be considered a disaster of unparalleled magnitude, since it has terminated in the annihilation of a whole people. Nevertheless, this is not a time for the indulgence of such useless sorrow. I rely upon my father's care to provide that these unhappy women shall be protected from injury, until the arrival of Arjûn, whom I have already dispatched my servant Dârek to bring to Duarka; and that Arjûn will soon be here, I have the fullest expectation. In the mean time I am compelled to leave you to repair to Balbehdder, who is anxiously awaiting my return. Twice has it been my destiny to witness the destruction of a whole race of people; first, that of the sons of Kourû, and in this last instance, that of my own peculiar tribe and people, the race of Jadou. Thus bereaved of my children and friends, it cannot be expected that I should ever again appear at Duarka; and my determination is therefore taken, with my brother Balbehdder, to retire into the solitude of the forests, there to devote the remainder of my days to the adoration of the Supreme. He had embraced his father's feet, and was about to depart, when his attention was arrested by a most piercing outcry among the women: a paroxysm of grief which he could only endeavour to appease by reminding them that against the will of God, and the dispensations of providence, all human remedy was unavailing; their only resource was resignation. As an inducement, however, to cease their lamentations, he assured them that Arjûn would be with them on the following day, whose presence would be sufficient to dispel every sorrow.

Having thus spoken, Krishna, bidding a last farewell to his father and all Duarka, quitted the place for ever, and returned to the spot where he had left Balbehddar. He observed that his brother continued seated, and resting against the tree in the same motionless position as when first discovered. But while he was thus looking on, he perceived an enormous white snake issuing from his mouth. The monstrous reptile exhibited on its appearance not less than a thousand heads, and making for the sea-shore, left Balbehdder a lifeless trunk under the shade of the Bur tree. Krishna further observed the sea assuming the form of a Brahmin, and coming to meet the serpent, which he saluted with expressions of ardent welcome. Innumerable serpents from the internal regions of the earth, such as Bassek,* and Kerkoutek,† and Beyrun,‡ and Pudma,§ and among others might be distinguished Dertarashet and Burrun,‖

* باسک † کرکوتک ‡ بیرن § پدم ‖ برن

this latter described as the genius* presiding over the waters, crowded also together to meet that form which must now be understood to have been the soul of Balbehdder. The white serpent, however, continued its progress into the sea, into the depths of which it finally plunged and disappeared.

Thus an eye-witness of the exit of Balbehdder, Krishna, a prey to sorrow, retired into a neighbouring forest district; and there seating himself upon the earth, with his head resting upon his knees, he ruminated at leisure on the course of these melancholy events. "The curse," said he to himself "which Kandahâry imprecated against, has at last overtaken me." He had been moreover forewarned, on some occasion or other, to be careful of the sole of his foot, because if any mischief ever occurred to him, that would be the direction in which it would come. These circumstances, we are told, have been noticed in the nineteenth Pourb,† or book of the Mahabharat. In conclusion, the whole race of Kouru, as well as that of Jadou, having been thus exterminated, Krishna said, that it now became his business also to quit the world.

Having chosen his place of rest apart on the Jungue, Krishna seated himself, laying one foot across his knee, and first bringing his soul and intellectual faculties to a common centre in the heart, he thence transferred them

* موکل † پرب

finally to the crown of his head. Such was the posture in which he had placed himself, when a hunter, with his bow and arrows, came accidentally to the spot; and at a little distance among the underwood, perceiving the sole of Krishna's foot, which rested across the knee, he conceived it was the foot of some wild animal, and letting fly an arrow, lodged it in the foot of Krishna; and here we are apprized that the point of this arrow was made from a portion of that identified wedge or piece of iron which had been discharged from the bowels of Samba, as described in another place.

Continuing to suppose that the object at which he had drawn his bow was some animal of the chase, the hunter ran up, and when he neared the spot, his astonishment must have been great, when, four-armed and clad in his saffron robe, the form of the immortal Krishna presented itself. Immediately throwing himself at the feet of Krishna, and explaining the nature of his fatal mistake, the hunter implored forgiveness. Krishna, with many soothing expressions, endeavoured to allay his distress, finally dismissing him with these words: "Go thy way, for thine is not the blame."*

It is here again stated, that the piece of iron which was the material of the fatal arrow-head was that which by order of Aukra Sing, the Rajah of Duarka, had been as far as possible reduced by filing, but the remnant of

* تاواني

which had been cast by the people into the sea. It so happened, that a fish should have swallowed this identical bit of iron, and the same fish being caught by some of the fishermen on the coast, was by them sold to the hunter; on opening the fish, the iron was found in its belly, and it was shaped by the hunter into the same arrow-head, which was thus destined to be fatal to the otherwise immortal Krishna.

On the departure of the hunter, a resplendent light arose from the form of Krishna, which diffused its lustre through the whole space from earth to heaven; and we are told by the poet, that on this memorable occasion the now expiring hero was attended by Ashwinikomâr.* the eight Pess,† the eleven Rudras,‡ the twelve suns, the forty-nine angels of death,§ the thirteen Basdeuas,|| together with Nâred, and innumerable Sidhas,¶ Kundrupas,** with Beswauss,†† and Chetter Sing, and other Apsara,‡‡ as well as Deutas or deified spirits of every class among the immortals, who now hastened to conduct the soul of Krishna to the abodes of the blessed. It is added, that the same light which shone over the house of his father Basdeu at the period of his birth, was that

* اشوني‌كمار — † هشت‌بس — ‡ ردر

§ موت — || بسديوا — ¶ سدهان

** كندربان — †† بسواس — ‡‡ اپسرها

Note that Kundrupas and Apsara are known to have been of the class of celestial spirits co-ordinate with angels perhaps.

which now illustrated the departure of Krishna, with whom it disappeared from the earth.

The celestial spirits who descended to become the escort of Krishna to the region of bliss, united to the utmost in enumerating the virtues of the hero, whom they thus attended to the sphere of Indra; by whom he was received with boundless joy, and conducted to the limits of his sphere of the heavenly system. Then Indra quitted him with the observation, that so far he was permitted to accompany him, but no farther; and Krishna was thus left to pursue his celestial course by himself.

Having, as formerly indicated, in concurrence with the orders of his master, made the best of his way to Hastnapour, Dârek, the charioteer, the moment he reached that capital, hastened to the presence of Rajah Judishter, in reply to whose interrogatories he briefly announced the entire destruction of the race of Jadou. So completely shocked was the Rajah by this intelligence, that he instantly swoöned away; but coming again to himself, he desired that Dârek would relate to him circumstantially all that he knew of this fearful disaster. Accordingly Dârek proceeded to describe without reserve all the circumstances of the fatal conflict, without omitting the curse of the Rehkkissers, in which it appeared to have originated, and thus terminating in the destruction of an entire race, consisting of so many renowned and illustrious branches. Rajah Judishter and his brothers listened to the dismal narrative with sensations of alarm, so much so, that although among the living they appeared like dead men.

Arjûn was the first to speak: he demanded of Rajah Judishter that he might be permitted to proceed immediately to Duarka, in order to ascertain the fate of Krishna and his father Basdeu, as well as the real extent of the disaster, and its consequences. This permission he obtained without difficulty, and he accordingly made the best of his way to the scene of the recent tragedy. On his arrival at Duarka, Arjûn found that city "like a widow mourning for the loss of her husband. Bereaved of the presence of Krishna and Balbehdder, and his other illustrious friends, it appeared to him overshadowed by a gloom far more appalling than he had been prepared to expect; and he could not restrain himself from giving loud expressions to his grief. At the same time the sixteen thousand and eight wives* of Krishna no sooner sat eyes on Arjûn, than they commenced all at once such piercing lamentations as filled the whole city with uproar and consternation, all having lost either husband, or son, or father, or brother, in the late catastrophe.

On witnessing this scene of mourning and woe, Arjûn seems to have yielded to despair, and for a time to have

* This number seems to bear some reference to the *thousand and eight* names of Krishna, being sixteen wives to each name, and one each to the surplus.

lost all powers of body and mind; but when he had continued in this state for some time, unable to determine in what manner to act, he at last in some degree was restored to his faculties, and he asked where it was that he should find Basdeu. The women directed him to the spot which the aged chief had selected for his abode. He was found by Arjûn in a reclining position, but the moment he saw him approach he arose, and Arjûn running to embrace his feet, the sight of his favourite friend brought to his recollection afresh the perfections of his heroic son. A paroxysm of grief ensued, and he was for some time unable to speak; neither could Arjûn restrain himself from lamenting aloud; and this coming to the ears of the women of Duarka, they rushed with hair dishevelled to the presence of Arjûn, and raised such a sorrowful outcry, as spread through the city such an example of distraction as the world had seldom, if ever, witnessed before.

After some time, the tears of Basdeu subsided in some degree, and he began to apostrophize with Arjûn on the loss of his friend. "Alas Arjûn," said he, "what is become of my friend—whither is the hero gone, who slew the wicked demons, and subdued so many puissant monarchs!" When he had been suffered, however, to indulge sufficiently in these ebullitions of grief, Arjûn ventured to ask if he could explain the cause which had produced such lamentable results—and he stated in reply that all had arisen from the senseless dispute between

Sautek, whom he designated as the disciple of Arjûn, and Kerretburma. "To the language employed between these two persons," said he, "is to be ascribed the total destruction of the stock of Jadou. Nevertheless, I am compelled to assert that the principal blame rests upon Sautek alone; since Kerretburma and the other combatants were inadvertently drawn into the fatal and unnatural conflict. It is, however, not to be forgotten, that although more remotely, the mischief had its origin in the malediction of the three Rehkkissers. Thus bereaved of my heroic son, the destroyer of so many oppressive demons, the conqueror of so many powerful sovereigns, of Kaunsa,* and Keissy,† and Seispal,‡ and Ahelkeb,|| and Kaljûn,§ my sorrows must be permitted to take their course; and although I know them to be unavailing, I yield myself an unrestricting victim to my griefs. From the time that he left me, I have neither eaten nor drank; but he assured me at parting that Arjûn would soon be with me, and would devote his attentions to my relief. Ever since have I been anxiously looking for thy arrival, and now that thou art on the spot, I cannot doubt but that thou will hasten to fulfil the instructions bequeathed to thee by thy lamented friend. These unhappy and afflicted women, together with the gold and jewels, and all the wealth and treasure which he left, are entirely thine to

* كنس † كيسي ‡ سيسپال
|| كالجون § احلكب

dispose of at discretion. As for me, after the loss of Krishna and Balbehdder, and so many other valued relatives and friends, it will be impossible, on my part, any longer to sustain the burthensome cares of this world."

Deeply affected by the wailings of the venerable patriarch, for such he must have been, Arjûn, when the agitation of his feelings would admit, replied in the following terms:—"Alas, my father, when Krishna is no more, of what avail to me will be the possessing of all this treasure; dost thou conceive that after he has been lost to us, either myself or my brothers will any longer continue to exercise the sovereign power, or any other of the functions of this sublunary world? This can never be—Krishna for ever lost, neither Judishter, nor Bheim, nor Nokkel, nor Sehdeu, nor Droopedy, will ever consent to bear a part on earth. For my brothers, and Droopedy, and myself, being as one person, their opinions will be just as mine; and be assured that the instant I return to Hastnapour, the cares of empire and all earthly concern will be for ever relinquished. "Go thou my son," at last said Basdeu, "look to the condition of those whom Krishna has left behind, and do with them as to thee may appear most expedient."

Invoking a blessing upon the aged chief, Arjûn then took his final leave, and calling for Dârek, proceeded with him to the palace of Krishna; where summoning together such of the ministers and other Brahmins of the household who had survived the recent carnage, they soon assembled in his presence. Here beholding before him all that remained of the adherents of his lamented friend, Arjûn burst afresh into expressions of sorrow, in which he was immediately joined by all present. At last one of the Brahmins, after reminding Arjûn that all these demonstrations of grief could not be productive of any useful effect, called upon him without further delay to fulfil the trust reposed in him by the departed Krishna.

Arjûn now announced to them that in seven days the whole city of Duarka would be overwhelmed by the sea. "Hasten then," said he, "to take those measures without loss of time that may enable you to quit the place at the shortest notice. Bring out your cars and elephants and horses, and every kind of vehicle that remains to you; and when ready, let them be loaded with your gold and jewels, and such other property as you may consider of most value. We must then make the best of our way to Indraprest* (that is Dehly), taking with us the widows of Krishna. There still survives for us one of the children of the departed hero, in Behrnaub,† the son of Anerdehah,‡ him also let us take along and establish in the sovereignty of Dehly. On the morning of the seventh day from this, and at the very instant we have quitted it, will the sea arise and swallow up the city; at your peril therefore be prepared for your de-

* اندرپرست † بحرناب ‡ انردهه

parture by the seventh day, for most surely shall all perish in the inundation that remain in the place on that day.

Arjûn passed that night in the palace of Krishna: and in the morning after the performance of his ablutions, when he was about to visit the aged Basdeu, his ears were all at once assailed by the almost deafening outcries, which issued from the residence of the venerable chief. These arose from the wailings of some thousands of women, who, with hair dishevelled, naked arms, and vestments torn, rent the air with their lamentations. Alarmed at the sudden uproar, Arjûn rushed into the street to demand the occasion. The people came running from the palace of Basdeu, announcing that, towards the latter part of the night, the father of Krishna had submitted to the hand of death; and that the outcry arose from his fourteen wives, including Deuky,* the mother of Krishna, and Rouhny,† the mother of Balbehdder, and numbers of other women, who were lamenting aloud over the lifeless body.

At the annunciation of this event, Arjûn experienced so painful a shock as nearly killed him, and he became for a short time insensible. From this state he was, however, soon awakened by the widows of Krishna, who called upon him to recollect that the crisis was too full of peril to indulge in useless regret. "Do that," said

* ديوكي † روهني

they, "which shall most speedily remove us from this devoted place, together with the body of Basdeu, lest something should occur to prevent our departure altogether; for we are not without our apprehensions that some outrage may be attempted against us, when once our enemies are aware of what has come to pass."

Without further delay, Arjûn repaired to the palace of the deceased, whose body he immediately directed to be conveyed, on the first instance, to the spot where, on some former occasion, Krishna himself had completed the august ceremonies of the Ashmeida Joug,* or grand sacrifice of the horse. Basdeu, when alive, had indicated the place to which he was desirous of being carried, and accordingly, in concurrence with this desire, Arjûn with his own hands lifted up the bier which bore his remains, and conveyed them to the spot thus indicated—where, the usual materials for cremation, sandal wood, wood of aloes, and aromatic oils of every description, having been prepared in sufficient abundance, the body of Basdeu was laid upon the pile, and four of his wives consumed themselves in the same fire.

Having thus acquitted himself of the last duties to the remains of Basdeu, Arjûn now repaired to that part of the coast where the race of Jadou had been destroyed by mutual immolation. There such a spectacle presented itself to his view, in the heaps of slain lying one upon another, as to excite his astonishment. When he had,

* اشیمدجگ

however, sufficiently indulged in some heart-rending reflections, he proceeded to give orders that the necessary quantity of fire-wood and oil should be collected together, and when all was ready, the bodies of such as he could recognise, such as Pandaman, the son of Krishna, with his brothers, and Sautek and Kerretburma, and Ekrour, and many more, were laid upon the pile and consumed to ashes. His next care was to send in search of the bodies of Krishna and Balbehdder, and these being found and brought to his presence, the pile of aromatic woods and oil was renewed, on which they were also consumed. He concluded the whole of these melancholy duties with the other usual ceremonies for the dead, and an offering of water to the souls of the departed.

Being then at leisure from these other cares, and the sixth day being now arrived, Arjûn gave orders that the whole population should immediately quit Duarka, and, as had been previously arranged, take the road to Indraprest; on which the whole of the surviving inhabitants, men, women, and children, with their slaves of both sexes, and every other individual belonging to it, came out of the city. Among these were the sixteen thousand wives of Krishna, each accompanied by a crowd of attendants, and others their relatives. The multitude was led by the son of Anerdehah, and grandson of Krishna, formerly adverted to and here called Bejernaum,* while Arjûn brought up the rear of the whole.

* بجرنام instead of بجرناب

On the very day on which Arjûn caused the city to be thus evacuated, the sea arose all at once, and in one stupendous wave, while the people from without were yet looking on at the appalling spectacle, rolling upon Duarka, in an instant overwhelmed the whole city and all that remained in it. Having witnessed this fearful catastrophe, the people became now alarmed lest the inundation might reach the spot on which they stood; and it was with some precipitation that they therefore commenced their journey, on which they proceeded until they came to the disemboguement of five rivers into the sea, where they encamped.*

It unfortunately happened, that the inhabitants of the surrounding territory were all highway robbers and thieves of the very worst description. Observing an encampment of such magnitude set up among them, and the greater part of its inmates composed of women, with an immensity of gold and jewels, and other valuable property, with few if any men for its protection, it is not surprising, that after consultation, they should have determined to plunder and make themselves masters of the whole. "Arjûn," said they, "is but one man, and what resistance can one man offer to the numbers that

* The present Duarka is seated on an island at the north-western point of the Peninsula of Gujerât, and was probably reduced to that insulated situation by some tremendous irruption of the sea, which may have furnished grounds for the tradition here repeated.

we shall bring against him!" Accordingly, collecting in great force, they poured into the camp, and proceeded on their work of violence.

In these circumstances, Arjûn stood before the plunderers, and, in a tone of derision called out to them, that as they came in safety, so they might depart—otherwise they must prepare to experience the well-known fatal effects of his famous bow. Perfectly regardless of what he said, the robbers continued their work of pillage, pouring into every part of the encampment, and carrying off all they could lay hands on. Some of the banditti now approached to attack the person of Arjûn, and the latter telling them that surely their hour was come since they disregarded his admonition, proceeded to string his celebrated bow, Kandeu.* What must have been his surprise and disappointment, when he found that with all his strength he was unable to bend the bow; and it was not until after a thousand exertions that he at last succeeded in bringing it within the string. But after fixing the arrow for discharge, his astonishment must have greatly increased, when he found with all his endeavours that he could not draw the bow. He now laid his hand upon his sword, and here again he was doomed to disappointment, for with his utmost exertions he was unable to disengage it from the scabbard.

The robbers were now close upon him, and each of them seizing a wife of Krishna by the hand, they were

* كانديو

carrying them off before his eyes into disgraceful bondage, when Arjûn became so overcome with indignation that he was about to kill himself. Again, however, he seized his bow, and after very many efforts, was at last able to draw it. Several of the robbers now bit the dust; but, contrary to former experience, which led him to expect that his quiver, through the influence of some supernatural agency, would as usual be replenished, he found that by frequent discharges he had expended every shaft. Arjûn in despair now rushed into the midst of the banditti, and smote them in different directions with his bow alone. The robbers were however in such numbers, that they continued, before his eyes, to cary off the women, treasure, and jewels, and every other description of property, almost without resistance. It was then, finding that all his efforts to prevent these deeds of violence and atrocity were unavailing, that Arjûn sat down to bewail the cruelty of his destiny. "Alas," cried he, "my fortune expired with Krishna."

In this extremity, lifting up his hands in prayer, Arjûn supplicated the most high for aid, and hence recovering some degree of strength and energy, he drew his sword and laid many of the banditti dead at his feet. Many of the women, all such indeed as remained uncaptured, were thus prevented from being carried away, and some part of the treasure and jewels was recovered. Having caused the whole to be reloaded, and remounted the women whom he had rescued from bondage, he conducted them as before, towards Hastnapoor and Indraprest, the ancient name of Dehly.

He proceeded now without interruption, and brought his charge safe to Gorkeiht.* He had bestowed some of the countries in his way upon the son of Kerretburma; and he now conferred the government of Gorkeiht, the territory about Panipet, then so called, upon the son of Sautek. Having performed certain religious duties, and bathed in the tank† at Gorkeiht, Arjûn soon afterwards came to Indraprest.‡ The sovereignty of this latter place, with its dependencies, as formerly proposed, was now bestowed upon the son of Anerdehah and grandson of Krishna, here designated by the name of Tchutter,§ or Betchutter.

Five of the wives of Krishna devoted themselves to the flames at Gorkeiht. These were Rokmeny,‖ Jamounty,¶ Sepahdra,** Semouty,†† and Kandahary,‡‡ the father of this latter belonging to the country of Kandahâr. Sethahâmah with some others of these widowed females, assuming the habit of the Senyaussies,§§ retired into the forests, where they devoted them-

* گرکهیت

† The lake of Tahnnaser, probably.

‡ Sometimes written اندرپست

§ بچتر ‖ رکمني ¶ جامونتي ** سپهدرا

†† سموتي ‡‡ کاندهاري §§ سناسيان

selves to the service of the deity, and of them nothing further was ever known.

Of the men who accompanied Arjûn from Duarka, he left the greater part with the grandson of Krishna, at Dehly; from whence, attended by a few others, he proceeded on a visit to Beyauss,* whom he found seated alone in a secluded corner. Having invoked a blessing on the head of the sage, he announced to him that he was Arjûn, come to offer his services. Beyauss told him he was welcome, and desired him to be seated. Perceiving that he was absorbed in some deep affliction, and that his complexion had undergone an extraordinary change, Beyauss demanded what it was that had befallen him, that nothing remained of the radiance which usually beamed on his brow. "Surely," remarked the sage, "thou hast had communication with some childless young widow, recently bereaved of her husband, or hast thou murdered a Brahmin, or basely fled on a contest with the enemy."

"Alas, my much venerated instructor," replied Arjûn, "of neither of the deeds to which thou hast referred have I been guilty; but that which has overwhelmed me with distress I am about to explain to thee. Krishna and Balbehdder have forsaken the world, and the race of Jadou, that warlike race so well known to thee, hath all perished in the waves of mutual immolation. Sautek, and Kerret-

* بیاس

burma, and Purdaman, and Gadheir,* with five hundred thousand more of that illustrious race have all fallen by each other's hands, who in this world had not their equal in courage and magnanimity. Still it would be as easy to convince me that they had dried up the ocean, or that the sky was fallen, or the mountains in motion, as that the immortal Krishna was dead.† Listen then further to the extraordinary things which I have to relate. I had brought with me the wives of Krishna to a place where five rivers enter the sea, when we were attacked by a body of robbers, who plundered us of our treasure and effects, and before my eyes carried off most of the women. I attempted to string my bow in order to kill the brutal plunderers, when to my astonishment I found that all my efforts to do so proved unavailing. Yet am I the same Arjûn that when Krishna preceded my car, by my skill in archery alone, broke the array, and entirely discomfited that host, which contained in its ranks such renowned warriors as Bheykempotâmah,‡ Derrounatchâreja,§ and Kerren.||

"In short," continued Arjûn, "such was the condition to which, by the departure of Krishna, I was reduced, that I was unable to contend with this band of misbegotten plunderers: for to the departure of Krishna can I alone ascribe the inglorious failure. I can only add,

* گدهیر

† The foregoing remark would seem rather to have come from Beyauss.

‡ بهیکم پتامه § درونا چارج || کرن

that bereaved of a friend like Krishna, I do not wish to live; and being determined no longer to exercise the functions of royalty, the object of my present visit is to advise with my venerated instructor as to the steps which in such circumstances I ought to pursue; command me then, my father, as to what I am to do."

Deeply afflicted by the relation, Beyauss replied to Arjûn in words to the following effect: "With regard to what has befallen the race of Jadou, that was, doubtless, the result of the Brahmin's malediction. But as to Krishna, that matchless hero who purged the earth of the presence of so many malignant demons, and their polluted followers of the human race, he is returned to that state of blissful existence from whence he came. For him, therefore, this mourning is superfluous. Neither is it to be denied, that exploits have also been performed by thyself and thy brothers, which have never been surpassed. But now that thy career of fortune has reached its close, it would well become thee to devote thyself to those pursuits that will ensure thy happiness in a future state. All things have their seasons, and hitherto has fortune been attached to thee and to thy race. That fortune is now declining, and the period is therefore arrived at which it would be prudent to abdicate the functions of earthly dominion. It was thy ascendant fortune, be it remembered, that furnished the means which enabled thee to achieve the discomfiture of such formidable opponents: but now being in the wane, it is not surprising, that thine efforts to bend thy celebrated bow, and to repel the outrages of a rude banditti, should have been unavailing. Wouldst thou, therefore, consult thine eternal welfare, let all further concern with the affairs of this world be abandoned for ever."

In continuing his narration to Rajah Jemenjah, Bishempayin proceeds to state, that when his conference with Beyauss came to an end, Arjun took a respectful leave of the venerated sage, and pursued his journey to Hastnapour, to the presence of Rajah Judishter, and his other brothers, who hastened to join him the moment they heard of his return. Arjun repeated from first to last all that had occurred in the consultation with Beyauss, and the Rajah and his brothers were equally affected by what they heard. It became, therefore, a subject of serious contemplation immediately to relinquish all concern with earthly grandeur, and all the cares of sovereign power.*

The historians of Hindustân, in prosecuting their narrative of these events, proceed to relate, that when Rajah Jemenjah had heard to the close, from Bishempayin, his detail of the carnage near Duarka, and his account of the demise of Krishna, Balbehdder, and Basdeu, he besought his instructor further to describe to him what were the steps taken by the sons of Pandu, on intelligence of these fearful disasters. In compliance with this request, Bishempayin states, that when Rajah Ju-

* Here terminates the sixteenth mystery of the Mahabharat, entitled موسل پرب *Moussil Purrub.*

dishter and his three brothers became thus apprized of the final destruction of the race of Jadou, and the departure of Krishna, the Rajah instantly determined on abdicating the sovereign power, and withdrawing from the world. In adopting this resolution, he observed to Arjun, that it was scarcely necessary to remind him that there exists in every period of time a peculiar influence in directing the affairs of life. "You say truly, "replied Arjun," whatever comes to pass is the work of time, and assuredly every period in time has its particular influence over human events. Thus, at one period, we were impelled to exercise the powersof royalty; but the influence now in operation urges us with irresistible effect, to discard the concerns of this world, and leave the country for ever." In this opinion, the whole of the five brothers concurred without hesitation.

Rajah Judishter then directed that they would send for Hejis,* the son of Dehtraushet,† and when he was come, calling for Rajah Purtchapet,‡ or Purrichet, the son of Abheiman, and grandson of Arjun, he took the diadem from his own brows, and placed it on the head of that prince, thus consigned to him the sovereign authority. He at the same time conferred the office of Vezzeir, or prime minister, on the above named Hejis, who was not inferior in birth to any one. After which, sending for Sepehdra, the sister of Krishna, wife of Arjun,

* هجیس † دهتراشت ‡ پرتچپت

and mother of Abheiman, he announced to her that this her grandson was destined to be a monarch of great renown, the dominions of both the houses of Pandu and Kouru having thus together devolved to him. The government of Indraprest and its dependencies had however been previously assigned to her nephew Betchetter, the grandson of Krishna; and he now admonished her to conduct herself towards him with the same spirit of harmony, as she must have seen to subsist between himself and Krishna—to repress every ambitious feeling that might actuate her to encroach upon the territory placed under his authority—to maintain with him a constant intercourse of friendship, and otherwise on all occasions to treat him with every mark of attention and respect.

After this the Rajah and his four brothers repaired to the Ganges, and therein performing their ablutions, poured out repeated libations to the memory of Krishna and Balbehdder, Basdeu and Purdaman, and the other sons and relatives of Krishna. Returning then to his palace, Rajah Judishter commenced a general distribution of food to the poor and needy, Brahmins as well as Tchettrias,—propitiatory for the souls of the departed worthies just mentioned. This was repeated for several days successively; after which, a donation of gold and manufactured goods, of cattle and horses, of elephants and chariots, and female slaves, to an amount beyond all calculation, was made to the same Brahmins and the indigent of every class.

Having acquitted himself of these demands on his munificence, Rajah Judishter sent to require the presence of Kerpatchareja,* and taking Rajah Pertchâpet by the hand, he solemnly committed him to the tuition of that celebrated sage, with the request that, as the preceptor and patron of his race, he would give to the young prince the same invaluable instructions in the art of war, and every other branch of science, as he had bestowed upon himself. He desired, at the same time, that he would consider the child as his own, for that, next after God, he had consigned the child to his paternal protection, in the full persuasion that he would not regret bestowing upon him every proof of kindness and affection. Kerpatchâreja cordially accepted of the charge, assuring Rajah Judishter that he should consider the young prince as much his own child, as he had formerly done with regard to Rajah Judishter himself: and peradventure with stronger claims on his attention, since the Rajah was going away, and leaving the child to meet his destiny alone.

These assurances on the part of Kerpatchareja gave ample satisfaction to Rajah Judishter, his brothers, and the two matrons Droopedy and Sehpedra. Having next assembled the Vezzeir, and other dignitaries and discreet personages of the monarchy, the Rajah announced to them that he had resigned his authority to his young

* كرپاچارج

relative, whom he now presented to them, in perfect confidence that they would yield to his successor the same proofs of zeal and loyalty as they had uniformly manifested towards himself. The announcement was received by all with a sensation of deep regret. They stated that of course they should not contend against the dictates of his authority, and that they were prepared to obey any one to whom he might think fit to consign them. "For this child," said they, "is he not already our superior lord, and how should we for a moment fail in our duty to him? But we have not yet been able to divest ourselves of the apprehension, that in thus abdicating the sovereign power thou art leaving us without a head." "My friends," replied Rajah Judishter, "hitherto it has been, indeed, my destiny to discharge the functions of earthly power, but my allotted period has reached its close. Henceforth my exertions must be directed to ensure by my deeds what may avail me in another world."

Then in the presence of all, taking the earrings from his ears, the enriched collar from his shoulders, the rings and bracelets from his hands and arms, the Rajah divested himself of his royal robes, and put on what was to serve for his future clothing, a doublet made of the bark of a tree. His four brothers, Bheim and Arjun, Nokkel and Sehdau, with their wife Droopedy, immediately followed the example, and putting off their splendid apparel and jewels, clad themselves also in the bark of trees. They then took the sacred fire which they kept in their houses for the purpose of sacrifice, and cast it into the Ganges, the whole population of Hastnapour, men and women, raising such piercing cries of lamentations and mourning, as surpassed all former example.

The Rajah and his brothers seemed, however, to rejoice at the change in their lot, and accordingly took their final departure from Hastnapour, accompanied by Droopedy, and followed by a single faithful dog. They were accompanied, at the same time, by the whole of the inhabitants, both men and women; of these, however, the Rajah and his companions took not the slightest notice, neither encouraging them to proceed, nor desiring them to remain at home. Observing, therefore, that the self-banished and illustrious exiles declined speaking to or taking any further notice of them, the people at last gradually dropped behind, and finally returned altogether to the city. Hejis, the Vezzeir, seemed determined still to attend them, but from this he was dissuaded by Kerpatchareja, through whose advice he also returned to Hastnapour. Abouny,* or Abouly, the wife of Arjun and daughter of Baussek,† walked into the Ganges, and disappeared: and Tchetterangdah,‡ the mother of Bebberbahn,§ went to reside with her son. The other wives of the five brothers remained under the protection of Rajah Purtchapet, at Hastnapour.

* ابولي † باسک ‡ چترانكدا § ببرباهن

It was about the rising of the sun that the sons of Pandu, with their wife Droopedy, commenced their pilgrimage, followed by the faithful quadruped. Rajah Judishter led the party, being followed in succession by Bheim Sing, Arjun, Nokkel, and Sehdeu, after whom went Droopedy, and last of all the dog. In this order they proceeded, directing their steps towards Bengal, until they came to the side of a talaub, or lake, on the extreme borders of that country, called the lake of Poust.* Here, while engaged in their ablutions, a form appeared to them in the likeness of a man, but in stature tall as a mountain, and the lustre of whose countenance spread a flood of light through all the space around. Approaching the sons of Pandu, the being announced to them that he was the *element of fire;* and that it was for his gratification Arjun, on some remarkable occasion, had preserved the forest of Kandehn,† until he thought fit to consume it with his own breath. "Now," continued he, addressing himself to Arjun, "that thou hast withdrawn from the world, give to me thy bow Kandeu and go wherever thou wilt." He further apprized them that the Tchukker, or Tchakra, of Krishna had already been deposited here. It being then agreed by the brothers that the bow was no longer of any use to them, Arjun threw both bow and quiver into the lake, and the form immediately disappeared.

* پوست     † کاندهن

The illustrious wanderers now turned south into the countries of the Dekhan,* and having traversed the whole of those regions, they came to the territory of Gujerat.† Having also visited every object of devotion in that country, they came to the place where once Duarka stood: and when Arjun exclaimed, "Here once was Duarka," the whole broke out into bitter lamentations.

Their course was next directed towards the country of the four rivers, the Punjaub,‡ and continuing their progress from thence northward, they came to the mountainous range in that quarter, and finally to Mount Himautchel.§ Proceeding thence they passed another mountain entirely composed of sand, after which they arrived at the mountain of Semirparbut.||

Here casting their eyes behind them, they beheld that Droopedy had sunk to the earth. On this Beim demanded of Rajah Judishter in what this unfortunate woman could have offended, that she should have been thus separated from her friends? The Rajah replied that there was nothing with which to reproach Droopedy; but she had one fault: although equally bound to each of the five brothers, she gave the preference to Arjûn, whom she loved the best of all, and hence it

* دکهن † گجرات ‡ پنجاب

§ هماچل formerly called Sewalik.

|| سمیرپربت

arose that she was condemned to be thus separated. With pitiless indifference the brothers left their once loved Droopedy thus abandoned to her fate. Some days afterwards they were proceeding on their pilgrimage, when suddenly Sehdeu also dropped to the earth. To a question similar to that which had been put with regard to Droopedy, Judishter replied, that Sehdeu had neither guilt nor blemish; but that he had the vanity to conceive that in science, particularly in astronomy, he was without his equal. With the same indifference they had shown towards the hapless Droopedy, they now abandoned their brother to his fate.

They had not, however, proceeded much further, when, with the same suddenness as had happened to his former companions, Nokkel fell to the earth. "Alas," exclaimed Bheima, "this brave youth was distinguished for every virtue that can adorn the character of man, and for faithful zeal in the service of his elder brother he had not his equal. Why is it then that he has thus untimely fallen?" "His fault," said Judishter, "consisted in thinking that, in personal beauty he was unrivalled." The brothers, however deeply affected, without saying a word more, and with the same indifference to the fate of their companion, as before, continued their journey.

There remained now the three brothers and the faithful quadruped which had followed them from the beginning. Suddenly, the heroic Arjun sunk to the earth.

"Alas, my brother," cried Bheim Sing, "an untruth never fell from the lips of Arjun, and in other respects how numberless were his virtues! what untold blemish was it that has condemned him also to this fatal separation?" "Thou hast spoken truly," replied the Rajah, "this our heroic brother, excepting in one point, was a faultless being; with his bow in hand, he thought the whole world did not contain his match; and he had the vanity to boast that, if he chose it, he could at any time, in a single day, consume his enemies in any number. For this arrogant opinion it is that Arjun also has met an early fate." With the same unpitying indifference as on the former occasions, the two surviving brothers quitted the form of Arjun, and went their way: but they had not proceeded far, when, like those who were gone before, Bheim fell to the earth, crying aloud to Rajah Judishter that he also had fallen, and stating it as his last request that he would explain to him wherein it was that he had offended, that he also should be thus torn from the society of his brother. "Alas, my brother," said Rajah Judishter, "thy vice consisted in being an enormous eater, and in conceiving that in bodily strength thou hadst not thine equal. Therefore it is that thou hast fallen."

Rajah Judishter was now left with no other companion than his dog; and he was proceeding, as before, on his journey, when he beheld coming to meet him on the road the god Indra, seated in his car, formed of precious stones of transcendant beauty. Indra invited him to ascend the car, observing that he would conduct him to Soorg,* the abode of the blest. " Until this sorrowful moment," replied Judishter, " my brothers and myself have been inseparable, although for the present they have one by one been lost to me. To ascend to heaven alone, leaving them on earth, I can never consent. If thou wilt condescend to take them along, I am prepared to accompany thee; otherwise, where they remain, there shall be my abode." Indra announced to him in reply, that his brothers were gone before, and, together with Droopedy, awaited his arrival in heaven: and moreover, that he was about to convey him to those blessed abodes, in the very form and body in which he then stood. The Rajah expressed himself satisfied; " but," said he, " this dog is my servant, and I shall take him with me." " Where I am about to convey thee," said Indra, " this dog can have no place; and there, where thou art going, thou wilt thyself immediately become a Deuta;† leave, therefore, the dog where he is." " How can I accede to any such thing," replied the Rajah—" The dog has served me faithfully for many years, and I cannot now consent to desert him; unless, therefore, thou art willing to take the dog along, leave me where I am, for while I have life I will never forsake him."

" I cannot forget, that in the catalogue of crimes there are four that exceed all others in enormity; first, is that

* سرگ    † دیوتہ

of delivering over to his enemies the man who has sought and obtained your protection; second, is the murder of a woman; third, is that of taking by force that which is the property of another; fourth, is to betray your friend. I could add a fifth, which I consider of no less magnitude; that which leads a man, in reckless disregard of the claims of faithful servitude, to abandon his servant in distress. This faithful quadruped is vitally devoted to me; for when, in the course of my painful pilgrimage, friends and brothers all forsook me, he alone remained to the last, to share my fate. To ascend to heaven alone, and desert him at such a crisis, would be in me an act of baseness to which I could never reconcile myself—only consent to take my dog along, and I am prepared to attend wherever thou art disposed to lead—if not, cease to trouble me, and leave me where I am."

Bishempayin here explains to Rajah Jemenjah, that the dog which was the subject of all this discussion, was no other than Dehrrem* (Virtue) or Charity, which had assumed this form, in order to accompany and make proof of the moral rectitude, fidelity, and benevolent spirit of Rajah Judishter, and had hitherto eluded the discovery of even Indra himself. Now, however, he had witnessed the last decisive proof of the Rajah's determination to forego the bliss of heaven itself, rather than desert his dog, he resumed his proper form and addressed

* دهرم

the Rajah in the following terms: "A thousand blessings be upon thee Rajah Judishter, for thy numberless and inestimable virtues, but more especially for that inflexible integrity which has borne thee safe through every trial. For well and rigidly hast thou been tried, and I thank thee that I have found what I sought for. Once before I appeared to thee, and that was in the form of a ram,* at the period when, with thy brothers, Jerjudehn expelled thee from thine house. When, also, thy four brothers were among the slain, and I asked thee to determine which of them I should restore to life, and thine election was in favour of Nokkel, notwithstanding the pre-eminence of both Bheema and Arjun, it was in that form that I stood before thee." This we are informed is all circumstantially related in that chapter or book of the Mahabharat entitled the Pourrub benn.† "That was one occasion," continued the genius of virtue, "on which I put thee to the proof; and this on which, rather than separate from thy dog, thou hast refused to accompany Indra himself to heaven, is the second, and I pronounce that there is no one like thee." Dehrrem had been now recognized by Indra, who besought his forgiveness for not having sooner recollected him.

After this Indra and Dehrrem and Ashnikomâr,‡ with others of the Deutas or Demigods, proceeded to place

* جچي either a ram or a hare.

† پرب بن ‡ اشني کمار the physician of the gods.

Rajah Judishter in the car of Indra, in which they now ascended towards the realms above. Having continued their celestial course for some time, they perceived that Nâred was approaching them, and him they all saluted with becoming respect. On this occasion that mysterious personage did not hesitate to pronounce, that of all the sovereign princes, and devout and otherwise illustrious individuals that ever trod the earth, the merits must have been inferior to those of this Rajah Judishter; since not one among them all ever attained to the signal privilege of thus ascending to heaven with the same body and form as he had animated on earth. Upon this, placing his hands together in a posture of supplication, Judishter besought of Nareda, Indra, and the other Deutas who accompanied him, to take him to the place where his brothers had gone before him; for if they took him to any other, be it good or be it bad, he would not remain there.

Indra thought fit to remind him that the world which he now saw was widely different from that which he had left, for here he was not permitted to wish for the presence of his brothers. "This," said he, "is a state in which we are akin to nothing but the immaculate essence of the ever-living Supreme, the fountain of all purity, and the dispenser of all good. Here, accordingly, it is not for every one to arrive, but for those alone who are the objects of his favour; and here thy brothers cannot come."

Still Rajah Judishter continued to expostulate with Indra. "All I ask," said he, "from the Almighty Supreme is, either that I may be permitted to take my brothers with me, or if not unworthy of such goodness, that they may be conveyed by any means to the same place with myself. If, on the other hand, they are considered unworthy of such favour, I can only implore, that wherever they may be, I may there be sent: for where my brothers and Droopedy are not present, I cannot taste repose."*

Those who have undertaken to transmit to posterity the events of this history, proceed to relate, that in his conference with Bishempayin, Rajah Jemenjah now besought him, since he had announced the reception in Soorg of the sons of Pandû, to say, as he doubtless well knew, and he, the Rajah, was anxious to learn, where it was that Jerjudehn and his brethren had taken up their abode in the other world. Bishempayin states in reply, that when Rajah Judishter was carried to heaven, one of the first objects that met his eye, was the same Jerjudehn seated on a throne, his countenance beaming with radiance like the sun, and numberless Deutas or demigods sitting around. At such a spectacle, Rajah Judishter could not suppress his indignation, and he was turning away, when the Deutas by whom he was accompanied demanded the cause. The Rajah replied, that

* Here ends the 17th mystery of the Mahabharat, entitled مهاپرسان *Mahapursan*.

he should not go to the same place with Jerjudehn—that guilty person, for whose gratification a whole world had been consigned to mutual slaughter—on whom the ties of blood had so little influence, that he could drive himself and his brothers, however nearly akin, to be helpless wanderers in the wilderness. These were injuries, he said, that had no parallel, and that nothing should induce him to enter, much less abide in the same place with Jerjudehn. "Take me," continued he, "O take me to the place where my brothers repose."

Nâred, who was one of the blessed spirits by whom he was still accompanied, cautioned Rajah Judishter to beware of such speeches, for this was not a place where malignant passions were permitted either to be indulged in, or to be borne in remembrance. "Jerjudehn," said he, "is a personage of such pre-eminent grandeur, that even the Deutas do homage to him, and the glory to which he has been admitted, is not greater than they are entitled to, who die on the field of battle. In short," concontinued Nâred, "here no remembrance is retained of what passed on earth between man and man: what passed on earth remains there still, but here animosities have no abode."—"If Jerjudehn," rejoined Rajah Judishter, "has been permitted to obtain an abode in bliss, where then are my noble brothers, all of whom were men of truth and matchless virtue? My sole anxiety is to visit those brothers, and my other heroic friends and relatives—to behold again the countenances of Kurrun, and Sautek, and Dreshtahdaman,* and the sons of Droopedy, Abheiman and Sehkundy, and those of Dreshtahdaman, as well as of the Rajahs Drooped† and Beyraut.‡ Shew me where they are: for where they are not I can have no abiding place. But more especially am I desirous of seeing the heroic Kurrun."— "Be it so," observed the attendant Deutas—"come on and thou shalt see them all."

Nared now led the way, followed by Rajah Judishter, when most unexpectedly they fell upon a track of the very vilest description, involved in darkness, covered with mud and clay, with human hair and flesh and blood scattered in all directions, while the sense of smelling was assailed by the most offensive and loathsome odours. He beheld also a great fire and hideous reptiles gnawing at the bodies of human beings—iron wheels§ for torture in great number—he beheld also numbers of human forms whom they were torturing with instruments of fire of various descriptions, and some of whom they cast into iron caldrons of boiling oil. There were also trees of fire to which they suspended those whom they were employed to torture.

Agitated to the last degree by the horrible spectacles thus presented to his view, Rajah Judishter demanded wherefore it was that they had brought him to this abode of misery? The Deutas who preceded now turned

* درشته‌دمن † دروپد ‡ بیرات § کنرهاي اهن

to him and said, that if he wished to see his brothers this was the way by which he must go. The Rajah declared that by that way he would go no further; and he was accordingly turning back, when all at once the voices of his brothers and Droopedy smote his ear, expostulating with him in the following terms: "we had rejoiced in some degree in the hope that by thy presence we should at last have been delivered from this fearful place—leaving us thus, whither wouldst thou go? while thou art present they cease to torment us." Recognizing the well-known voices of his relatives, the Rajah stood fixed to the spot, and demanded who they were that could be condemned thus fearfully to suffer? They then repeated one by one aloud the names of his brothers and Droopedy, and in short of all his relatives. "Alas!" cried Rajah Judishter, "what might have been the offence that could have brought upon you such tortures as these? It is to me not less strange than unaccountable to witness what I have seen, in the state of bliss and glory to which Jerjudehn has attained, whose whole life was one course of guilt and wickedness—and my brothers in this state of suffering, who trod without ceasing in the paths of virtue, and whose undeviating study it was to do that which is acceptable to Him who is the fountain of purity, and supreme over all existence. Can this then have been the work of celestial spirits, such as you are?" Then further addressing himself to the Deutas, by whom he was attended, he said—" Is it then through you that Jerjudehn, whose deeds on earth are so well known to all; should have obtained such a place in glory, while my blameless brothers and unoffending relatives are thrown into the state in which I find them? Leave me where I am, for hence I will never depart." And in this resolution he continued inflexible, however urged to the contrary by the Deutas. They accordingly left him seated where he was, and returned to the presence of Indra; to whom they related what had passed, stating the stern and positive refusal of the Rajah to accompany them.

Indra, attended by the whole of the Deutas, now hastened to the place where Rajah Judishter had been left, when all at once the fire, and the various means of torture, with those that suffered under their infliction, entirely disappeared; and, in the midst of the Deutas, stood the personification of virtue, Dehrrem, in its most attractive form, addressing the Rajah in the following terms: " Thrice, O Rajah, have I now put thy virtue to the proof, and thrice hast thou been found worthy of applause. The first time was when I appeared to thee in the form of a *Tcheitcha*—the second, when I accompanied thee in thy pilgrimage in the form of a dog—and the third time is that, in which I have thus revealed to thee the torments prepared for wicked men." Indra then also addressed Rajah Judishter, assuring him that by these proofs of unshaken virtue, he had filled the Deutas with universal joy—that to all monarchs it was allotted once to visit the region of condemned souls.* He that sees affliction may depart in joy: and he that at first meets with something of delight, may ultimately find his way into the place of torments. That the Rajah's portion in sin having been indeed extremely small, it was considered a sufficient atonement, that he should for a short time have been condemned to view, without partaking in the torments of hell, and for that purpose the frightful scenes he had witnessed had been laid before him. " At the period thy brother Bheima slew the elephant, whose name was Ashutahama,"† said Indra, " it was thy boast to thy preceptor, Derrounatchâreja, that the hero of that name had been slain; which induced the sage to think that he had lost his son. Now as there existed in this a semblance of falsehood, so has it been assigned to thee as an atonement, to contemplate what bore the resemblance of hell, and its punishments—in which it appeared to thee that thy brothers and thy wife, Droopedy, were partakers: and thus finally hast thou been absolved from the stain of sin and guilt."

" Come now with me," continued Indra, " and I will conduct thee into Soorg, that abode of the blessed —there thou shalt behold the disembodied spirits of all those heroes who died with thee in the conflicts of

* دوزخ

† اشوتهاما Ashutahama was the name of the son of Derrounatchâreja as well as of an elephant, in the Mahabharata. D. P.

the field of battle, and who have gone before thee to Heaven; and these are now seated in the abode of Kurrun—of Kurrun the offspring of the sun, whose abode is now amidst the radiance of his father's beams. For the great sacrifice, the Ashmeidajoug, also performed by thee on earth, this reward will be in full proportion. The monarchs who before thee have been the benefactors of mankind, the authors of all acts of benēficence, such as Rajah Hurtchund,* Rajah Mandehâta,† Rajah Bhagirat,‡ and Bharat,§ the son of Dhekent,‖ have all attained the most exalted state of glory, and for thee also is reserved a similar state of glory and perfect felicity. By this passage it is that we communicate with the earth; but whoever bathes in yonder stream,¶ puts off the form of man, and assumes that of the Deutas, or demigods."

Rajah Judishter and the Deutas now approached the bank of the sacred Ganges; in which having bathed, he found on coming out of the stream, that he had put off every vestige of the human form, and put on that of the Deutas, or deified heroes. His countenance assumed a radiance like that of the sun, and he was completely purified from the influence of anger and envy, and all the malignant passions incident to the nature of man in his mortal state. After this transform-

* حرچند † مان‌دهاتا ‡ بهگرت § بهرت

‖ دهکینت ¶ The Celestial Ganges.

ation, he was invited by the Deutas to accompany them further on.

He proceeded accordingly, admiring, as he was carried along in these several blissful abodes, the disembodied spirits of departed heroes, and other approved servants of the Most High, until he came to the place where he beheld Krishna in his four-handed form, holding in either hand respectively the Tchukker or Tchakra, [perhaps thunderbolt] the horn,* the mace,† the mysterious gem,‡ and the Pudma.§ Near his divine friend stood the heroic Arjun; and on one side he beheld Kurrun surrounded by twelve suns, or luminaries like suns. Near the genius, or spirit, which presided over the winds, he beheld the warlike Bheim Sing; and Nokkel, and Sehdeu, he beheld in the society of Ashounikomaur.‖ On inquiring for Droopedy, the Rajah was now apprised by Indra, that that illustrious female was in reality the goddess of fortune,¶ who, on his account had assumed the human form, and who in consequence of an invocation by Mahadeu,** was born in the palace or family of a certain Rajah. "As to the five sons," continued Indra, "of whom she became the mother, there they are all standing near her." The Rajah looked accordingly, and beheld the five sons of Droopedy

* موق the conch shell.

† كرز ‡ جواهر § پدم

‖ اشوني‌كمار ¶ دولت ** مهاديو

standing behind their mother. "Your uncle Dehrtoraushat," resumed Indra, "was of the celestial order of Kundaroups,* behold him standing there;" pointing to a particular space in the heavenly region, "and as to the Saudha† and Deutas, and thy kindred the whole of the Jadous, from whatever stock derived, there they all are reposing in the various places allotted to them."

"Abheiman," continued Indra, "we know to have been the offspring of the moon, and there he appears accordingly in the same mansion with his sire; with regard to thy father Rajah Pand, both he and his wives Konty‡ and Maudery§ have been allotted an abode with me. Bheykempotaumah having been born of one of the eight *Bess*,|| he will at present be found where they are. Some of the sons of Kourû were the issue of a Kundaroup and some of a Rajihs;¶ some also derived their birth from a Jejah, or *Jetcha*.** And accordingly all of that race who may have fallen in battle will be found in communion with the stock from whence they sprung."

When Bishempayin had proceeded thus far in his narration, Rajah Jemenjah interposed to remark that in mentioning the names of so many illustrious personages, it seemed strange that he should have omitted those of

* كندريان † سادهـ ‡ كنت

§ مادري || بس ¶ راجهس

** جچ Whether this be a ram or a hare is doubtful.

the Rajahs Drooped and Beyraut, as well as of Kehrougah,* the son of Bheim Sing, of Derberrat Keit,† of Tcheit Sing, of Rajah Setheit,‡ and of many others that appeared to have escaped his notice. "The same questions," replied Bishempayin, "which you have now proposed to me, was formerly urged upon Beyauss by certain Rehkkisers, and the answer of Beyauss shall be mine to you on this occasion."

Beyauss stated that certain mysterious beings had occasionally appeared on earth through the medium of an Outaur, Avataur,§ or descent, for some benevolent purpose known to the Most-High alone. These, when they had continued on earth as long as was necessary to the designs of the Supreme Being, terminated their mortal existence, and returned to the place from whence they came. Of these Derrounatchâreja was an Avataur, or incarnation of Purhusput,‖ and on earth acquired the sciences peculiar to that divine personage. As soon, therefore, as his years came to a close, he returned to that state from which he had been taken. Purdaman, again, who was an Avataur of Sonnetkomaur,¶ Dehr-toraushet of a Kundaroup, and Rajah Pand with his two wives, were all united in the communion of Indra. Rajah Drooped and Rajah Beyraut, with Derreshekeit** and Tcheit Sing and Oukra Sing, and Basdeu,†† and

* کهروک
† دربرتکت
‡ ست حیت
§ ادتار
‖ پرهسپت
¶ سنتکمار
** درشیکت
†† The futher of Krishna.

Krishna, and Anerdehah; all these latter were incarnations of Basdeva. Jerjudehn is in communion with Kaljoug, and Shikken with the Duapra. Budder and *Rajah Judishter* are in the communion with Dehrrum, the personification of Virtue. Balbehdder was the Avataur of Seihggah Nag,* the serpent monarch, and is again united to the source of his Being.

The sixteen thousand wives of Krishna who drowned themselves in the river Sreswatty,† all ascended to heaven, and are united to the Apsara. Kehroura being of demon race is in communion with the Rajihs, formerly mentioned. The brothers of Jerjudehn, and others of those individuals whose names I omit to repeat, are gone, some to the sphere of Indra, and some to that of Burrun, the spirit which presides over rain.

The details of the Mahabharat afforded to Rajah Jemenjah the utmost delight; and having soon after concluded the ceremonies of the sacrifice in which he had been engaged, he dismissed the multitude of Brahmins and other pious mendicants who had thronged to the place, loaded with presents, to their several abodes.

It was by command of his instructor Beyauss, or Veiasa, that Bishempayin related to Rajah Jemenjah the whole of this eventful story from beginning to end; and the reason why the work in which it is contained received the title of the Mahabharat, is thus explained.

* سیکھہ ناگ

† سرستي

At a remote period there lived at Hastnapour a common ancestor of the sons of Kourrû and Pandu, whose name was Rajah Bahrat,* a monarch of such transcendent renown, that none who succeeded ever attained to such a pitch of glory, either in puissance or extent of dominion: and as the work related to the exploits of his descendants, the designation of Mahabharat was bestowed upon it.

One good effect to be derived from hearing the narrative is this. Whoever the Brahmin is that may listen with serious attention to this story from the commencement to the close, he shall in battle never be defeated. Another is, that a pregnant woman listening with similar attention, shall assuredly be the mother of a prudent and intelligent child. Whoever also shall faithfully read the contents of this work, such as they are, without variation, shall have the enjoyment of much good; while he that is even a simple hearer, and no more, shall for the most part enjoy a life of happiness, without ever being visited by any affliction of serious magnitude.

We are further informed that this great work of the Mahabharat was composed by the sage Beyauss himself, in the space of three years; that it is fraught with the jewels of meaning, and with details of rare and extraordinary interest, in infinite variety and number; and we are lastly assured, that whoever shall read this book of a

* بهرت

morning, bearing the attainment of any particular object in mind, will eventually succeed to his heart's content.

And, last of all, we are now told that the original work was translated from the Sanskrit* language into Persian, in the space of a year and a half, by Nekeib Khaun;† several Brahmins learned in the original having knowledge of the undertaking, and explaining to the *sinful* translator, in Hindy, regularly as they proceeded in the reading.

The Persian copy from which the above has been translated into English was finished on the eleventh day of the former month of Rabbeia of the 1126th of the Hidjira, corresponding with the 16th of March, A.D. 1714, being the 3d year of the reign of Furrukh Seir.

Translation by

*Brecon,* DAVID PRICE.

*25th of March* 1831.

* سهس کرت

† نقیب خان